LADON

MONSTERS OF MYTHOLOG

25 VOLUMES

Hellenic

Amycus
Anteus
The Calydonian Boar
Cerberus
Chimaera
The Cyclopes
The Dragon of Boeotia
The Furies
Geryon
Harpalyce
Hecate
The Hydra
Ladon
Medusa
The Minotaur
The Nemean Lion
Procrustes
Scylla and Charybdis
The Sirens
The Spear-birds
The Sphinx

Norse

Fafnir
Fenris

Celtic

Drabne of Dole
Pig's Ploughman

MONSTERS OF MYTHOLOGY

LADON

Bernard Evslin

CHELSEA HOUSE PUBLISHERS

New York   Philadelphia

1990

EDITOR
Remmel Nunn

ART DIRECTOR
Maria Epes

PICTURE RESEARCHER
Susan Quist

SENIOR DESIGNER
Marjorie Zaum

EDITORIAL ASSISTANTS
Nate Eaton, Mark Rifkin

3   5   7   9   8   6   4   2

Library of Congress Cataloging-in-Publication Data

Evslin, Bernard.
Ladon / Bernard Evslin.

p.   cm.—(Monsters of mythology)
Bibliography: p.
Summary: Retells the myth of Ladon, the enormous serpent used by
Hera to try to destroy Hercules.
ISBN 1-55546-254-5
1. Ladon (Greek mythology)—Juvenile literature.
[1. Ladon (Greek mythology) 2. Mythology, Greek]
I. Title. II. Series: Evslin, Bernard. Monsters of mythology.
BL820.L25E94   1989   398.24′54—dc20   89-34379 CIP AC

Printed and bound in Mexico.

For TANYA EVSLIN
halfway across the world, but very near

Characters

Monsters

Ladon
(LAY don)

An enormous serpent, the scourge of the sea and its islands

Gods

Hera
(HEE ruh)

Queen of the Gods

Ares
(AIR eez)

God of War

Aphrodite
(af ruh DY tee)

Goddess of Love

Demeter
(DEM ih tuhr)

Goddess of Growing Things

Artemis
(AHR tuh mihs)

Goddess of the Moon

Iris (EYE rihs)	Caster of Rainbows
Hecate (HECK uh tee)	Queen of the Harpies
Atlas (AT luhs)	A condemned Titan
The Hesperides (hess PEHR ih deez)	Daughters of Atlas, now apple nymphs
Hypnos (HIPP nohs)	God of Sleep, Master of Dreams

Demigods

Hercules (HER ku leez)	Son of Zeus, strongest man in the world
Iole (EYE oh lee)	Daughter of the Rainbow

Mortals

Thyone (thee OH nee)	A young Amazon
Nycippe (ny SIH pee)	Friend of Thyone, another Amazon
Hippolyte (hih PAHL ih tee)	Queen of the Amazons

Malo (MAH loh)	A poet
Nameless Poet	Nycippe's captive

Animals

Pegasus (PEG uh suhs)	A winged horse
The Silver Stag	

Contents

1

Food that Isn't Fish

ot long after things began, certain homeless gods were offered a garden called Earth where they might grow fruit and grain and flowers. Animals, too, were promised, and a special clever one who would look like a cross between ape and god, and be prone to the kind of misadventure that most amused the Mighty Ones.

At first, though, this new place was just a bowl of red-hot rock full of water that hissed and boiled and bubbled. Gods hunched above it, trying to peer through the steam. When the bowl cooled they saw that it held a vital broth. Powerful new life was sprouting, casting itself into a wild variety of shapes, which swam off and began making more of themselves. And when they weren't breeding they were eating. Down through the entire life chain, what was bigger fed on what was smaller. But creatures of every size bred so fast that there was always enough to eat.

During those earliest years when a few islands had thrust themselves out of the roiling tides, another form of life was slowly blossoming. When it appeared, even the gods were dismayed.

Monsters!

Deep undersea, enormous eggs cracked and the first monsters wriggled out. They began growing as soon as they left the egg, and reached full size in a single day. These huge misshapen beasts not only ate everything in sight but seemed to be of a different nature, seemed to kill not only for food but for pleasure.

Dread and Evil had entered the world—which was now ready for man to appear.

The first humans in the Garden of Earth found themselves among fruit trees, and fed upon olives and figs, quinces, pomegranates, and the rich seeds called nuts. All this kept them alive and healthy, but there was something else they wanted; they didn't know what. This craving led them deeper and deeper into the orchard until, finally, they came upon a tree that bore golden fruit.

Uttering glad cries they rushed upon the tree, tore fruit from the branches and crammed it into their mouths. It was so delicious and they were so happy to be eating it that they ignored the thing that was wrapped about the trunk in huge, green coils— or, perhaps, they took it for a thick vine.

It was not a vine. It was a serpent called Ladon, one of the first monsters, and the very first to crawl out of the sea in search of food that wasn't fish. On his way through the orchard he had eaten a stag, a bear, and a flight of wild geese, and still wanted more.

Obeying some instinct, he stopped hunting; he wrapped himself about a tree and waited for a meal to come to him. It came—a troop of naked men and women, all fresh and shining, and very hungry. He watched them eating fruit for a while, then began eating them.

When he was finished he fell asleep, still draped about the tree, but more tightly because he was fatter.

Islands kept rising from the sea; on every one of them animals began to breed, including men. Ladon swam from island to island, stalking the larger animals through field and wood, but stopping always at a village when he could find one, because he had formed a special craving for human flesh.

When he returned to the immense sea-cavern where monster eggs were hatched, he told his family about these new islands where the hunting was so good and the game was so delicious. And certain of his brothers and sisters followed him when he surfaced again. They crawled ashore after him and began to hunt.

These were his sister, Echidne, the sea viper; her son, the three-headed dog named Cerberus, who refused to eat humans and fed on wild boar; a cousin, Polypus, the sea blob, who had no jaws but simply dropped his jellylike mass on his prey and digested it alive; and Ladon's niece, the Sphinx, a winged lion with a woman's head. Once ashore, she discovered the use of her

He wrapped himself about a tree
and waited for a meal to come to him.

Hera's hatred festered and swelled,
filling her to the brim
with its venom.

wings, sprang into the air and began to hunt like a giant hawk, striking from above and devouring bears as if they were rabbits, and eagles as if they were doves.

But Ladon's parents, Ceto, the triple snake, and Phorcys, the sea hog, refused to leave the depths of the ocean. They didn't like the land or anything connected with it, and fed happily on sharks and octopi and enormous turtles.

Thousands of years passed—only a few months in the life of a god or monster—and islands were sliding together to form continents. On the most beautiful peninsula, where hills ran down to the Middle Sea, there stood a high mountain, called Olympus.

Upon its peak, Zeus, the King of the Gods, built his cloud castle, and dwelt there with his wife, Hera, Queen of the Gods.

But Zeus courted a young princess of Thebes, Alcmene, Lady of the Light Footsteps. She bore twins. One was the son of her husband; the other—a giant, shining babe—was the son of Zeus. She named this one Hercules. And from his infancy on, Hera hated him and vowed to destroy him. She couldn't kill him herself because Zeus favored the lad and would be most displeased.

So she employed monsters.

But Hercules slew the first two she sent against him—the Nemean Lion and the Hydra, each of whom had wasted their districts, devouring herds, herdsmen, villagers, and warriors. And with each of the young man's victories Hera's hatred festered and swelled, filling her to the brim with its venom.

2

The Harpy Queen

ades, Ruler of the Dead, also loathed Hercules and had taught his fiends and demons to do so. For by killing monsters the young hero saved the lives of mortals, depriving Hades of subjects, and the fiends and demons of those they might torment. So it was that Hecate, Queen of the Harpies and Hades' most trusted murderess, was often sent to the upper regions to confer with Hera—who welcomed her advice.

Hecate knew that it was Hera's habit to finish the day by strolling in the Garden of the Gods, when dusk bewitched the sight and the evening breeze was heavy with fragrance. The hundred-handed giant who tended the garden did his best to please Hera, who was very hard to please. Each day he wove her a different chaplet of flowers. And upon this dusk, as Hecate folded her brass wings and landed on the grass, she saw that Hera wore a crown of iris and rose and gentian. Soft flames of blue and deeper blue and crimson mingled in her dark hair.

Hecate gasped with pure pleasure. "That creepy gardener of yours has worked well today, O Queen. His chaplet of flowers burns upon your head more gorgeously than any wrought of jewels."

"I'm glad to see you, dear friend," said Hera. "I've been in a foul mood all day long."

"Any reason?"

"The same reason. The same damned thing has happened again despite all my efforts. Hercules has killed the Hydra and come out of the battle without a scratch. I can't understand how it happened."

"Let us reason it out together, My Queen. Reports of the battle have drifted down to us, remote as we are from your business up here. And from what I understand Hercules went in very well prepared. He was armored from head to toe in the hide of the Nemean Lion—his first kill, as you will remember—and that hide cannot be pierced by any weapon. Yes, his entire body was covered; he made leggings and boots of the hide, gauntlets too, and wore the lion's skull as a helmet. So he went untouched by the poison fangs of the hundred-headed monster. We must ask ourselves why this rash youth prepared himself so carefully this time."

"Any ideas?"

"I think someone is feeding him valuable information."

"You're saying my secrets are being betrayed?"

"Yes."

"By whom?"

"By someone you confide in. Someone close to you."

"I confide in almost no one beside you."

"Then the traitor should be easy to find. How about that creature who flits about on your errands?"

"Iris?"

"I mean the loony thing who flutters out after storms, flinging those stupid colors around."

"That's Iris, Caster of Rainbows, and my messenger."

"Does she know your secrets?"

"A few, perhaps. Not all."

"Something tells me she's the one," said Hecate. "She has a treacherous look. All smiles all the time, and soft words. No one can be that sweet."

"You just don't like her."

"Do *you*—really?"

"Well," said Hera, "I admit her sugary ways gripe me sometimes, but she's been useful to me."

"I think she's been even more useful to Hercules."

"As it happened, I kept her close to my side before the battle. She wasn't out of my sight for a second. There was no way she could have gotten to him."

"Couldn't she have sent anyone?"

"She has a daughter," said Hera. "Impudent, nosy brat. I suppose she could have sent her. But I can't believe she'd dare to. She knows what would happen if I found out."

"If I were you I'd start making it happen," said Hecate.

"I can't—not yet."

"Why not?"

"We have no hard evidence of her guilt. If I do dreadful things to her out of mere suspicion there will be an uproar in Heaven. She's a general favorite up here, you know."

"I'll go digging for evidence, My Queen. I'll visit the grove at Lerna and try to find someone who actually saw the battle."

"No people would have been there," said Hera. "Mortals fled the very name of the Hydra."

"Birds would have been in the trees or flying overhead," said Hecate. "Birds make excellent witnesses. And I know how to question them. They trust me because I have wings."

3

Flight of the Rainbow

In a great meadow in Arcadia dwelt a clan of flower nymphs. It was their task to gather wild blossoms and steep them in a vat, making dyes for the rainbow goddess. Iris visited the meadow before every storm, dipped her streamers in the dyes, then, when the storm was finished, flung them across the sky in an arc of colors.

The flower nymphs were her most trusted friends. She left her child, Iole, in their care. And here the tiny girl had grown into a lovely, long-legged one, supple as a sapling.

Now, upon this blue and gold day, the nymphs were surprised to see Iris floating down. "Greetings!" one cried. "We did not expect to see you today. The sky is clear and the wind is from the west."

"Another kind of storm is brewing," said Iris. "I'll explain later, dear friends. Right now I must speak with Iole."

She drew her daughter aside. "What is it, Mother?" cried Iole. "You look so serious. Oh, I know, I know!"

"What do you know?"

"You've learned that Hera is planning a new peril for Hercules, and you want me to warn him. Well, I'm ready. I've been longing to search for him anyway, but had no excuse."

"Well, my child," said Iris. "It is we who face peril. Hera suspects that we helped him against the Hydra. We must flee."

"Where to?"

"Anywhere . . . everywhere. She'll ransack every corner of the earth, and the seas also."

"But we move lightly and swiftly, Mother. And know how to melt into thin air or merge with the shadows. So perhaps we can elude her."

"Perhaps, but we must separate," said Iris. "If we stay together she'll surely find us. You go one way and I'll go the other. And we shall meet in better times, my darling."

"I'm ready. Farewell."

"Farewell, lovely child. Kiss me."

They embraced. Wept a tear or two. Then smiled bravely at each other, kissed again, and parted.

Iole fled so lightly over the meadow that the grass didn't bend beneath her feet. She disappeared into a fringe of trees, singing as she went. Released from her mother's care, she could now search for her beloved Hercules. And this made her very happy.

On brass wings Hecate flew back to Olympus, and alighted in the Garden of the Gods. It wanted an hour till dusk—Hera's time to walk in the garden. And Hecate amused herself by taking a twig and scratching lines in the damp earth. An idea had struck her for a new torment to be called the Marrow Log, and she was sketching its design. When she saw Hera coming she flung the twig away and arose to greet her.

"I've done it!" she cried. "I have the proof we need. It was indeed Iris and Iole who betrayed you. Iris overheard our conversation about the Hydra's poison fangs and sent her daughter to warn Hercules that he must wear lion-skin armor."

"How did you find out?"

"I caught a flower nymph and tortured her a bit. She wasn't much fun. I'd hardly gotten started before she yammered out all she knew."

"Very well," said Hera. "Let's go catch them. We'd better hurry, though. Iris may suspect something. She can read my mood even at a distance."

"I'm ready," said Hecate.

Hera whistled up her swan chariot. In a rush of white wings the great birds drew the chariot to the garden. Hera jumped in. The swans beat their wings again and the chariot arose. Hecate spread her wings and flew easily alongside.

They sped high and low, searching sky and earth. They dipped into the valleys, searched the slopes, skimmed the treetops. Hecate descended sometimes to question birds. But search as they might, they could find no trace of the rainbow goddess or her daughter.

4

A Suitable Monster

era prowled the mountaintop, raging. "What's the use of being Queen of the Gods if I'm thwarted every place I turn? I can't punish Iris or Iole because I can't find them. Nor can I find a suitable task for Hercules. Since he slew the Hydra, monster activity has slowed down to a crawl. All the best serpents and dragons and spear-birds and giant boars seem to be stuck in their holes or dens or undersea caverns or wherever the hell they lurk . . . This can't go on. Surely, somewhere, there's some powerful, murderous beast I can use. But I hear of no countryside being ravaged, no crops uprooted, no herds devoured, no villagers massacred. And that muscle-bound young lout is lolling at his ease somewhere, safe from my vengeance. It's unbearable! I simply must find a suitable monster and arrange a fatal encounter."

On impulse she whistled up her chariot and ranged over the Middle Sea from the southern shore of Attica to the northern edge of Africa. For the most dreadful monsters, she knew, were to be found in the sea.

Flying west toward Iberia, she saw a three-decked ship running before the wind. She watched it idly as the wind dropped and the sail flapped, causing the men to spring onto the rowing benches and unship their long oars. The oar blades flashed and

The serpent flexed until its head was level with the deck.
Then it opened its jaws. . . . Hera heard
the hull cracking, heard muffled screams
as the men vanished.

the ship crawled over the glittering water. Then she saw something else.

A huge, wedge-shaped head poked out of the sea. Coil upon coil, the impossibly long body of a serpent heaved out. The head swiveled toward the ship; its loops flattened and it began to swim after the vessel. It seemed to be gliding through the water without effort, yet it was catching up to the ship.

The sailors hadn't seen it. They kept rowing, and sang as they rowed. Hera had dipped her chariot closer and could hear them sing. But the song turned to wild yells as the serpent cut in front of the bow and began to uncoil. Up, up it went until it towered above the mast. The men had cast away their oars and were wielding swords and spears and axes.

The serpent flexed until its head was level with the deck. Then it opened its jaws, and the horrified seamen were looking down a hundred yards of gullet, lined with teeth. The jaws closed over the entire ship from stem to stern. Hera heard the hull cracking, heard muffled screams as the men vanished.

The serpent lifted itself slightly again and spat out mast, oars, cordage, weapons, bits of sail. The debris floated in the reddening water. The serpent slid under and was gone.

"Magnificent!" cried Hera. "That's the monster for me! I must find out more about him."

She returned to Olympus and sent a message to Tartarus, summoning Hecate, who came immediately. This time Hera re-

ceived the Harpy queen in the courtyard of the cloud castle, and described what she had seen the day before.

"Sounds like Ladon," said Hecate.

"Tell me about him."

"He's the son of Ceto and Phorcys, and of all the monster brood is probably the most powerful. Uncoiled, he would stretch higher than that cedar. And his jaw hinge is located near his tail. While hunting in the sea he seeks whales because of his size but, as you have seen, will swerve away from a pod of whales to chase a ship."

"Yes, yes!" cried Hera. "And when his jaws closed he was crunching the ship—mast, oars, sails, and all. It happened too fast for anyone to escape. He swallowed the whole crew and spat out the wood. Not a man was left alive. I saw it happen, O Hecate, and the darkest closet of your Hell can offer no sight more stimulating."

"We have our moments," drawled Hecate. "You haven't visited us lately. We've added an interesting torment or two."

"Forgive me, dear. All I can think of at the moment is Ladon. What a splendid beast—exactly what I need for Hercules. I can just picture those wonderful long jaws closing on that misbegotten cur. Chomp . . . gulp . . . nothing left but a bloody rag of lion skin and some splinters of oaken club. I can't wait."

5

Another Hunger

Iole was wandering through a wood. She heard voices raised in terror—yelling, shrieking, sobbing. Moving swiftly as a cat she climbed a cedar that towered over the other trees, so that she was able to look down past a fringe of willows into a clearing where a village stood.

There she saw a serpent with huge, gaping jaws. He lay in a circle. His lower jaw rested on the ground; his upper jaw was lifted high, high. With his tail he was sweeping people into his mouth. He had encircled the entire population of the village, had eaten most of them, and was now finishing the rest. When the last one was gone, he spat buttons and bits of cloth, then carefully arranged his bulging coils and went to sleep.

"What a brute!" said Iole to herself. "I hope Hercules hasn't heard about it. Because my brave darling thinks he's been put on earth to protect people against monsters, and he'd surely challenge this one. But it's too big even for Hercules . . . Makes the Hydra seem like a tangle of earthworms . . . It's gorgeous, though, in its own horrid way. Those mottled leather coils, green and yellow, like patches of sunlight on the forest floor . . . Is it awake? Yes . . . It has very big eyes for a snake. I can feel the heat of them. It's a male, I think. Is he looking at me? He is! I wonder if he's still hungry? How could he be, after that meal! . . . I'm not afraid. I refuse to be afraid. I've always liked snakes, and they've always liked me. That cobra who used to visit the meadow—the flower nymphs were scared, but I used him to jump rope with. Perhaps this one would be friendly, too . . ."

Snakes have no eyelids; they can't blink. And Ladon very much wanted to blink. Something absolutely strange was happening high up in the cedar. Like all reptiles, tiny or monstrous, he was color-blind; things were different shades of gray to him.

But it was the mission of Iris to blazon the sign of the gods' occasional mercy across the heavens. When she hung her rainbow, she mixed a magic in its colors so that they might be visible to all creatures who walked, flew, swam, or crept. Iole had inherited this gift without knowing it. Her own colors blazed, banishing grayness, and came to Ladon now not only as a wonderful dance of light, but as a fragrance of flowers; more than that—almost like the maddening odor of game when he was famished; but different from that too, quickening another hunger, one he had never known.

He wanted to blink, but he couldn't. He wanted . . . wanted . . . He wanted to enter that weird dazzling and take what it held—that red-gold fall of hair, those green eyes, those ivory-bronze arms and legs. His entire length shuddered with dread and delight.

Ladon was in love.

Iole saw the serpent unwind himself. His lower coils stayed where they were; the upper part of him glided across the clearing, through the willows, toward the cedar. She saw him slide up the tree. He came halfway up. The great leather wedge of his head was weaving near the soles of her feet. His eyes stabbed into hers. They seemed to whirl, making her dizzy. She clung to the branch but did not look away from him. She did not wish to show fear.

"Greetings," he said.

He wanted to blink, but he couldn't.

His voice came as a huge rustling, chopped into words.
"You're not a person . . . What are you?"

"Demigoddess."

"I am Ladon."

"My name is Iole."

"Iole . . . "

"*Oh*-le, not *you*-le."

"Will you marry me?"

"No."

"Why not?"

"Don't want to."

"Why?"

"Just don't."

"Can we be friends?"

"Well . . ."

"Why don't you like me?"

"You eat in an unkindly way."

"Unkindly?"

"You kill first."

"No. I prefer live meat."

"That's even worse."

"No live meat, no dead meat. What can I eat?"

"Things you don't have to kill."

"Like what?"

"Grass . . . hay . . . stuff that cows eat, and sheep."

"What I do is wait until a cow or a sheep has its meal, then I eat the cow or sheep or buffalo, or whatever. That way I get my meat and greens at the same time."

"Your meat eating doesn't stop at cattle, sir. You've been eating people."

"Mmm . . . delicious. Easy to catch, too."

"That's why we can't be friends."

"Just because I eat people?"

"That's right."

"What do you care what happens to them? You're a goddess."

"Only half—on my mother's side. My father was a mortal man. And I can't be friends with anyone who eats human flesh."

"When would I have to stop?"

"Immediately."

She saw him slide up the tree. He came halfway up.

"That's very soon. Can't I sort of taper off?"

"Absolutely not! Bad habits must be stopped immediately, or they go on and on and on."

He stared at her. She stared back. She was very young, but woman enough to know that she must not cool his ardor by telling him she loved another.

"What are you thinking about?" he asked. "Stop thinking. Just say yes."

"To what?"

"That you'll marry me."

"We're quite different, you know."

"Well, you're trying to change me. If I stop eating people that will make us less different. And we can go on from there."

"Anyway, I'm too young."

"Much?"

"A few years, I guess."

"What's that? Nothing at all. I'm thousands of years old. Been here from the beginning, you know. Seems now as though I'd been waiting for you all the time."

"That's sweet," she murmured.

"So I can easily wait a few more years. But you must stay with me while I'm waiting. Or I'll get impatient."

"Will you stop eating people?"

"I'll just browse on that putrid herbage, I promise. Come down now. You can ride on my neck."

"You're almost totally neck, aren't you?"

"I mean just behind my head. You'll be comfortable."

"Then what?"

"We'll go anywhere you like. Cruising, perhaps. Would you like to go to sea? Would you like to visit the underwater cave where my family lives?"

"Are they monsters?"

"Certainly, purebred."

"Will they like me?"

"Who can help it? Besides, they won't dare not to. I'm the eldest son."

Hera, walking in the garden, saw a tall, green-clad figure approaching her. It was her sister Demeter, Goddess of Growing Things.

"Greetings," she said. "It's rare that one sees you in the time of harvest."

"Yes," said Demeter shortly. "I understand that you take an interest in Ladon."

"What of it?"

"I must ask you to restrain that gluttonous beast. He's been ranging up and down the land, devouring my crops. He can consume a wheat field in a single day, or finish off an entire orchard. All the Boeotian harvest has fled down his maw. Now he's starting on Thessaly. I won't stand for it."

"Barley Mother," said Hera, "you must be mistaken. That serpent is totally carnivorous. He touches nothing that is not meat."

"Once, perhaps. Not now. He's fallen in love and turned vegetarian."

"I don't believe it!" gasped Hera.

"Believe it, Sister. Why would I be saying this if it weren't so?"

"What vile enchantress has tamed that splendid ferocity?"

"Oh, you know her well," said Demeter. "It's Iris's daughter—Iole."

A windy dusk had flowed over the garden. The first pale stars were printing themselves on a great blowing lilac sky. Hera's screech of rage made them shiver on their axes.

6

The War God

res, God of War, needed hours of violent exercise before he could speak politely to anyone. Since Aphrodite was coming to visit him that afternoon, he spent the morning with a wild bull he had just added to his herd. It was a magnificent animal—huge, pure black, with coral nostrils, ivory hooves, and polished ivory horns. It had been sent as a gift by a tribe of Ares' most ardent worshipers, the women warriors of Scythia, called Amazons.

Ares knew that he had to teach the beast some manners before introducing it to his cows. The way to do this, he thought, was to master the bull on its own level—that is, by fighting it as if he, Ares, were a rival bull.

They were on a grassy meadow on a plateau north of Olympus, where Ares grazed his herds and trained his horses. Wearing nothing but his helmet, Ares circled the bull, crouching, moving very slowly. The bull simply turned as Ares circled, watching him always. Ares was patient. Again and again he circled the bull, until its eyes became holes of red fire and it began to paw the ground.

Suddenly, it charged. It bowled terrifically over the grass, a throbbing mountain of muscle, driving its sharp horns with enough force to pierce a stone wall. Ares stood his ground. He lowered his head, hunched his shoulders, and took the shock full on. Now the forehead of a bull, the space between its horns, is a heavy ridge of bone, solid as iron plate. And this frontal bone dented itself against Ares' helmet. One horn grazed his shoulder. Blood spurted.

But his legs were planted like tree stumps: He was immovable. The bull shook its head and trotted off a few yards. Blood streamed from its rubbery nostrils. Ares twisted his neck to look at his own bloody shoulder. Gods do not have red blood like humans. What runs in their veins is called *ichor*. It is pink and has a fragrance like fermenting honey, and clots very quickly, healing its own wound.

Swiftly, the bull moved again, hooking under now with one horn, trying to stab it into Ares' belly and rip his entrails out. Ares caught the horn, caught the other horn with his other hand, and vaulted between horns, landing on the bull's back. All in one motion he whirled, raised his rocklike fist, and slammed it down in a spot just in front of the bull's hump and in back of his skull.

The bull staggered, but did not fall. Ares slid off. He watched as the bull staggered a few more steps, then righted itself and turned to face him. The fire was gone from its eyes. It was too proud to admit defeat, but did not claim victory, and did not attack. It dropped its head and began to graze. And Ares knew it was fit to meet his cows—just as he himself was now, drained of rage, and calm enough to show courtesy to Aphrodite.

He heard her laughter. He turned and saw her. In the heat of battle he had not seen her coming. She had hidden behind a bush and had watched the whole thing. She flowed across the meadow, still laughing. She reached up, took the helmet from his head, and kissed the last drops of ichor from his shoulder.

"What a splendid beast," she said. "Where did you steal him?"

"I didn't."

"No, of course. You are Ares. You do not steal, you take."

"Wrong again."

"Purchase? Never!"

"It was given to me. A gift from a grateful congregation. From the Amazons, thanking me for granting them success in battle."

"Those wild women, eh? What a crew."

"Finest cavalry in the Middle Sea basin. And considered quite attractive by those who like their women big and fierce.

Swiftly, the bull moved again.

*She looked at him in a way that said,
"Tell me your idea and
I'll say it's wonderful,
no matter what I think."*

As for me, I admire them, but would rather court a she-bear. Let me dive in the river. I'm too sweaty to converse with the most beautiful creature on Earth, or in Heaven."

"You're so nice after you fight," she murmured. "So dreadful before . . . Go take your swim. I'll be waiting."

Some time later, they were lounging on a grassy bank near the river. Aphrodite was singing softly . . . a song dedicated to her by a poet named Thallo, who dwelt on Helicon.

"Very nice, I suppose," grunted Ares. "But I have absolutely no ear for poetry."

"I know you don't, dear."

"Tell you what, I don't care much for those who churn out the stuff, either . . . Gabby, worthless lot . . . D'you know those Parnassus and Helicon fellows praise every god except me? They don't do Hades much either, but me even less. Not one single solitary verse. And they praise nongods too. Reams of stuff about those they call heroes. And yes—here's the sickening part of it: They'll praise warriors also, and feats of arms, and victories— and never a good word for me, who goes to all the trouble of starting those wars."

"You're working yourself up again, dear. And I don't think that bull's ready for another go yet. You'll have to wrestle a couple of bears, or something."

"Never mind, I'm serious now, and—hey! I've just had a great idea."

She looked at him in a way that said, "Tell me your idea and I'll say it's wonderful, no matter what I think."

He said nothing. He was gazing out across the river and there was a growl of laughter in his throat.

"When he laughs like that," thought Aphrodite, "it means someone's about to suffer. Or some city or some nation. I don't think I want to know what that idea is."

7

An Amazon's Dream

hat dusk, Ares visited Lemnos, where dwelt Hypnos, God of Sleep. He was the son of Night, little brother of Death, and father of Dreams. He lived in a cave with his wife, Aglaia, most brilliant of the Graces. Outside the cave was a garden where the poppy grew, and the lotus, and other flowers that compel sleep.

Ares came with gifts: a necklace of jet and pearl for Aglaia and, riding his wrist like a hawk, an enormous black eagle with unwinking yellow eyes. "This eagle," he said to Hypnos, "will draw your chariot more swiftly across the sky than you have ever traveled before. That way you'll be able to crisscross the night, dropping more dreams than ever."

"I thank you, Brother," said Hypnos.

"But you know," said Ares, "when I bring gifts I ask favors."

"Name it," said Hypnos.

"I wish to send a dream to Scythia."

"To whom in Scythia?"

"To the strongest young filly among the Amazon tribe."

And he told Hypnos what he wanted the dream to do.

"I need a hair of your head and a drop of your blood," said Hypnos.

Ares pulled a hair from his head and squeezed a drop of ichor from the wound on his shoulder that had not quite healed.

"Now I can make your image appear to her," said Hypnos. "And I promise you she will dream so vividly that she will be up at daybreak to ride on your mission."

The lives of the Amazons were so entangled with the lives of their horses that they gave themselves horse names. Hippolyte, the name of their queen, means "horsebreaker." Melanippe means "black mare," Leucippe, "white mare," and so on. The young girls, those who had to chop their own wood, and cook their own food, and wash their own clothes, because they did not yet have a man to do these chores, were called "fillies." Big, sleek, powerful girls they were, bursting with health, full of restless energy because they had not yet ridden out on a husband-raid.

The tallest and strongest and swiftest of these was named Thyone. She had pale brown hair, almost silver in a certain light, and gray eyes. Lying now in her bearskin tent she seemed to glimmer as she slept. Hypnos slid in, and stood looking down at her. He stepped into her sleep, wove a colored dream, and glided out.

It was Ares she saw. He was clad in brass armor, and stood on a cloud, raising a fiery spear. His voice, when he spoke, was war cry, spear-shock, and the clang of shield against shield.

"Thyone," he said. "Do not wait for the next husband-raid. Go out alone. Mount at dawn, ride to Mount Helicon. There, among a rabble of poets, you will find one named Thallo. He is to be yours. Bring him back and work him hard."

The voice ceased. The image faded. Thyone woke up. Knowing she had to arise at dawn, she tried to go back to sleep. But she could not. She was afire with eagerness and curiosity and unanswered questions. She came out of her tent and ran to that of her cousin, Nycippe, a blonde spearwoman of the First Troop.

She stopped outside the tent and made wolf noises, two soft howls and a snarl—the signal of her clan, meaning, "Come quickly!"

Nycippe's hair gleamed in the pale starlight as she slipped out of the tent. "Thyone! What do you want?"

"I must talk to you."

"Can't it wait till morning?"

"No, no . . . listen!" She clutched Nycippe's shoulder, and poured out the tale of her dream. " . . . So I must obey him, Cousin. I ride at dawn."

"You don't want a poet," said Nycippe. "My sister had one and he was very lazy. Get yourself a herdsman or a fisher-lad or something—someone used to hard work."

"I can't. Ares clearly said I was to bring home a poet."

"Well, you'd better start training him on the way back, so he'll be ready to work when you reach your tent."

"Good idea, I guess."

"But be careful. Men are more fragile than we are, and poets even more so. They bleed easily. So don't use a whip. And don't use a stick. You might break his bones."

"How, then?"

Grinning, Nycippe held up her big palm. "This way, dear, hard and frequent."

"Really? Over my knee?"

"Three times a day, more if he needs it."

"Is that how you do yours?"

"At first, but I use a hickory switch now. He doesn't need much beating anymore. He's learned what I expect and what he'll get if I don't get it."

"How about that poet? Your sister still have him?"

"Traded him for a donkey. Caught herself a woodsman and is much happier."

The girl left Nycippe's tent, confused and excited—too worked up to get back to sleep. So she whistled up her mare and was on her way before dawn.

8

Thyone Goes Hunting

hyone was riding her mare up a slope of Helicon. Far above, a stallion trumpeted. She searched the heights but saw no horse. Again she heard the trumpeting, seeming to come from directly above. She looked up, startled. There in the sky, balanced on golden wings, was a magnificent white horse. From tales she had heard she knew it was Pegasus, the winged steed belonging to the Muses, whom generations of bards had tried to ride.

He bugled again. Thyone felt her mare trembling. She tethered her and climbed a winding path. She had expected to see a mob of haggard, hairy creatures strumming lyres and humming to themselves. But the place seemed deserted. Finally, she saw someone perched on a rock, gazing up at Pegasus.

She approached and stood above him. He was slender as a weasel, with dark, curly hair and a pointed beard. Curious eyes, tilted like a goat's, filling with yellow light as he looked up at her.

"Do you know someone named Thallo?" she asked.

"We all know one another here."

"Where can I find him?"

He smiled at her,
but did not move.

"You can't. He's holed up somewhere trying to finish some tedious epic. Take him all summer, probably."

"I'll go dig him out of his hole."

"What do you want him for? Did you commission some verses? Actually, he's nowhere near as good as people say. *I'll* write you a poem. I'm much better than people say. Any subject, two drachmae a line. Discount, over fifty lines. Be twice as much for anyone else, but I always make a special price for goddesses."

"You take me for a goddess?"

"Certainly. You're Artemis."

"Are you sure?"

"Recognized you immediately—so tall, so silvery, bearing bow and arrows. You're the moon, come at noon. See! I'm rhyming already. How about it? Two drachmae a line. Forget about that old has-been. Take me."

"I'm not Artemis, little man. Not a goddess at all. And if I take you you'll have no time for writing."

"Not write? What will I do?"

"You'll be taught your duties soon enough. Come along."

"Where to?"

"Scythia."

"Oh, no, too cold. Freezes the ink."

"What's your name?"

"Malo."

"Come along, Malo."

He smiled at her, but did not move. She swooped, swung him off the rock, tucked him under arm, and trotted to where her mare was tethered. Amazons rode into battle bareback, but used a saddle when traveling so that they could hang their gear. She was about to fold him over the withers of her mount, then remembered that her water bag would have to be refilled for the journey home. This meant that she had to leave her captive and find a spring. She stretched him on the ground, face down, pinning him under her big bare foot, as she unlooped a rope from the saddle. Kneeling, she trussed him like a calf, then lifted him again and carried him into the shade of a tree.

She found a spring, filled her water bag, and hurried back. From far off she saw a tangle of ropes under the tree. Long legs flashing, she raced like a deer to where she had left him. He was gone! She heard his voice, and whirled about. He was plucking grass and feeding the mare, talking to it softly.

In two steps she was upon him—swung him off the ground,

Long legs flashing,
she raced like a deer
to where she had left him.

lifting him until his face was level with hers. "How did you get loose?"

"I was a deck boy once. Learned about knots. I can slip any bond."

She set him down but kept his shoulder clamped. "Why didn't you run away while you had the chance?"

"Run away—after being captured by the moon? Flee the light? What kind of poet would do that?"

Her grip tightened on his shoulder as she bent to him. His eyes were dancing. "Are you mocking me?" she growled.

"Would I dare?"

"I'm not a goddess, I told you."

"How do you know? It's the worshiper who decides. Let's

not go to Scythia, though. Vile climate. We'll stay here. I know a nice vacant cave on the south slope."

"You *are* mocking."

"No, my silvery huntress, no."

"You're too clever for me."

"And you're too big for me. But we can work things out."

She sat on a rock and lifted him into her lap. "Show me," she murmured.

9

Artemis in Scythia

ews travels fast on Olympus, twice as fast if it's spiced with malice. And there were many who delighted in telling the haughty Artemis that a tall, fleet, lovely Amazon had come to Helicon and was being worshiped as a goddess. Every bard there had dropped all projects to sing her praises. At first they kept comparing her to the moon goddess, but now declared that she was more beautiful.

Enraged, Artemis flew to Helicon. She hovered invisibly, observing everyone, getting angrier all the time. She was about to descend and slay them with her silver arrows, but remembered Zeus's decree forbidding any god to kill more than six mortals a month.

"Never mind," she said to herself. "I can contrive a more painful vengeance."

She flew then to Scythia, coming to earth on a vast plain where stood the bearskin tents of the Amazons. It was a busy scene. The tall young women milled about—breaking horses, practicing archery, disciplining their men. A rich clamor filled the air: the neighing of horses, swish of arrows, meaty thwack of hand against husband, women yelling, dogs barking, men sobbing.

*It was a busy scene. The tall young women
milled about—breaking horses,
practicing archery . . .*

Artemis spotted the one she was looking for, the largest woman, almost middle-aged, very stately, wearing a crown. It was Hippolyte, the Amazon queen. The goddess made herself visible, appearing before Hippolyte in all her brightness.

"Come into the glade," she said.

"I am your servant," said the queen.

"I bring you news of Thyone."

"Thyone! Our silver filly! She went a-raiding and vanished. We thought her dead."

"Not dead. Wed.."

"What?" cried Hippolyte. "A wife?"

Artemis then told her what she had seen on Helicon. ". . . And she's living very contentedly in their cave, hoping to bear his child."

"Then she really loves him?"

"Certainly seems like it."

"But he's so very small, you say."

"Very tricky, too. Knows how to transform handicaps into attractions. He uses his smallness."

"I don't understand."

"He works up close. And has convinced her that his exact size is the ideal of manly beauty."

"Goddess, are you really telling me that this runt has so befuddled our proud young filly that she's doing unwomanly house chores?"

"Just the heavy work. Chops wood, lifts things that are beyond his strength—which are most things. She does the hunting, of course. He does the cooking. He's good at it."

"Well, it's all too disgusting," said Hippolyte, "and cannot be permitted to go on. This Malo must be a wizard of some kind, and has bound her with vile enchantments."

"Indeed . . . he can weave a spell with words."

"Our sister must be rescued, and those evil ones taught a lesson. We'll ride to Helicon and finish them off. Keep a few of the biggest, perhaps, and kill the rest."

"I must warn you," said Artemis. "She'll fight like a tigress to protect him. You'll have to kill her too."

"If necessary, we will," said Hippolyte. "Death before dishonor."

Hypnos was the kindliest of the gods, and could not forget the dream he had brought to Thyone. He knew that Ares had meant mischief, but didn't know what kind. So he decided to keep his eye on things.

As it happened he had much business over Helicon. Poets use up dreams at an alarming rate, and don't always wait until they're asleep. So Hypnos overflew Helicon every night, and was

It was Hippolyte, the Amazon queen.

pleased to see that Thallo was unhurt, and that the young Amazon was living happily with someone else.

But then he learned that Artemis had begun to hate the Heliconians even more than Ares did, and was mobilizing the Amazons for a murderous raid. He fretted about this. But he was of a very peaceable nature, and never opposed anyone in anything.

Finally, though, he decided to do something in his own way. "It will take a truly heroic effort," he said to himself, "to keep those wild women from wholesale bardicide. They'll simply mangle the poor poets unless they're stopped. But who can help? No god will take the trouble, and the Muses need a year to make up their minds about anything. It will have to be a mortal. But who? . . . Hercules, of course! He is the one most willing and most able to help the weak against the strong. I'll do a dream for him this very night."

10

Hecate's Idea

otanus, the hundred-handed giant who was the gods' gardener, traveled the world over seeking the most exquisite blooms so that he might bring them back to Olympus. He was now showing his latest cuttings to Hera.

"Yes, very nice," she said.

He told then about a very curious plant he had discovered in a distant jungle. "Gorgeous, My Queen. Something like an orchid, but evil. Twice a day, at dawn and dusk, its blooms open—then snap shut on whatever insect or small bird is sipping its pollen."

"Does it eat them?"

"It does, it does."

"Are there any large enough to eat men?"

"Not that I know of. The ones I saw were orchid size."

"Well," said Hera. "You'll oblige me if you can find some really big ones. I'd like to give a bouquet to someone."

Just then Hera heard a shout from above, and turned to see Hecate coasting in on brass wings. The giant sidled away. For all his size he was afraid of Hecate. The Harpy queen ran toward Hera, shouting.

"Good news!"

"About time," said Hera. "What's happening?"

"Fortune, which favors the fortunate—namely us—has called poetry to our aid."

"I don't have the slightest idea what you're talking about."

"As it happens, Hercules is on his way to Mount Helicon, where the Muses dwell. He's on one of his absurd missions of mercy—to rescue some oppressed bards. They're always whimpering about one thing or another, you know."

"How does all this help us?"

"Listen carefully," said Hecate. "We shall manage the weather and clamp a great heat on Helicon when he gets there. So he'll be very thirsty and drink deeply of the pure crystal waters of the Hippocrene Spring, which casts those who drink it into a gentle frenzy. They believe their own visions and grow drunk on the music of words. In short, the hero you loathe will be transformed into an apprentice poet. Bits of verse boiling within him will slacken his warrior fibre. His wits will be addled. He'll lose muscle tone, and his reflexes will falter, then vanish. So he should be easy prey for Ladon."

"Don't speak to me of Ladon!" cried Hera. "I've told you he's useless now. He's slobbering over that redheaded slut. It's absolutely disgusting."

"No, it's good."

"Good? What can you possibly mean?"

"I mean," said Hecate, "this unlikely love affair can play into our hands also. I have thought the matter through, O Hera—forward and backward—and I have a further idea, one that will bind things together so that we may solve all our problems at once."

"Sounds like fantasy," said Hera. "But please tell me. I need something to lift my spirits."

"We'll get word to Iole that Hercules is on Helicon. She'll hurry there, and Ladon will follow, for he can't bear to let her out of his sight. When she sees Hercules she'll rush into his arms, of course, and this—mark my words now—this will make the serpent madly jealous. He'll forget all that vegetable nonsense and attack Hercules, who, weakened by poetics, will be unable to defend himself."

"Sounds all right," said Hera glumly, "but a lot of things do till you start doing them."

"You'll feel better when we go into action," said Hecate.

"Where shall we start?"

"The first thing is to get word to the wench about Hercules' whereabouts. She's at sea, probably, with her snake. Your brother, Poseidon, can help us here. He has shoals of gabby Nereids who can spread the news."

"I'll send him a message immediately," said Hera.

She did. Poseidon spoke to his Nereids, who fanned out, jabbering to each other. Now gossip spreads even faster underwater than on land. And before long, Iole, who often dived off Ladon's head to frolic with sea nymphs, learned that Hercules was visiting Mount Helicon.

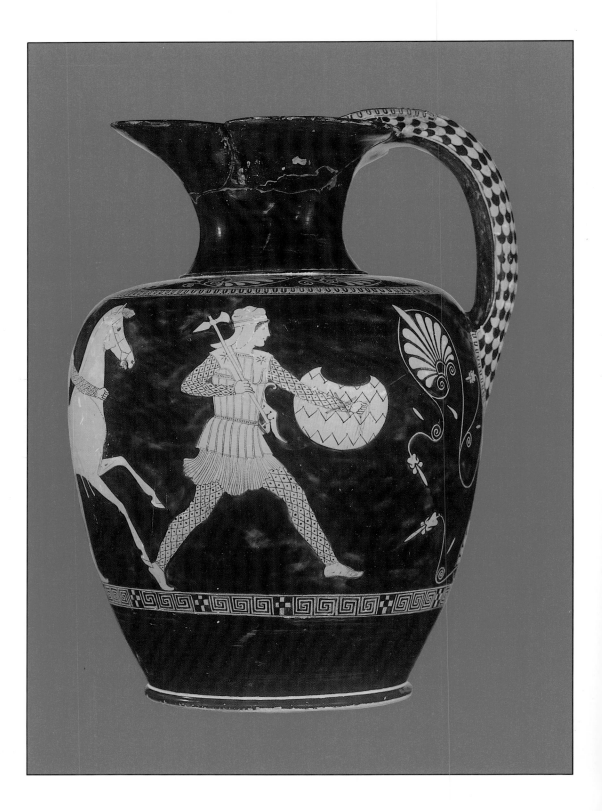

11

The Raid

Awaking from the night-vision sent by Hypnos, Hercules knew that a mountainful of poets was in dreadful peril. He didn't quite understand the nature of the threat, but knew that he was being called on to help. Whereupon he set off for Helicon, beginning a journey that was to cover more distance than he thought.

But the Amazons were already on their way, riding swift horses, while Hercules went on foot. So the warrior women reached the mountain before he did. They climbed until they reached a grassy plain cut by a stream. Here, Hippolyte called a halt.

"Hearken, sisters," she called. "Dismount and let the horses drink; then proceed on foot. Fan out and comb the slopes. Those you hunt are on their home ground and know every hiding place. They'll dive into holes, wedge themselves in hollow trees, and burrow into caves. But I want them taken, every last one."

"Do we kill them on the spot?" called one girl, unfurling a whip. "Or can we have some fun first?"

"Neither," cried Hippolyte. "This will be our collection point. I want them all brought right here so we can sort them out. There may be a few we'll want to take home. The others you can do with as you wish before finishing them off. But I want them all here first, cleaned up and ready for sorting. The Second Squad will be the scrubbing detail. Take 'em downstream for their bath, and scrub hard; they're a filthy lot, I hear. Better burn their clothes too, or we'll catch fleas. That's it, ladies. Good hunting!"

Yelling and laughing, the girls ran up the slope. Each bore bow and quiver as well as a length of rope, or a net. Long-legged and effortlessly fierce as storks hunting frogs, they fanned out in a skirmish line as they raced up the mountain.

The stream purling swiftly downhill formed a natural pool at the end of the meadow. Here was where the captives were to be bathed. While waiting for the first men to be brought in, the girls of the scrub detail flung off their tunics and dived into the pool. Singing and laughing, they cavorted in the cool water; they were sleek and powerful as dolphins.

Nycippe was stalking through an oak grove. Somewhere in the wood men were screaming, which meant they were being captured. But she hadn't caught anyone yet, and itched for action. She felt a sudden craving for something sweet, and began to search for honeycombs. She found a hollow tree and reached in—and touched something alive. It moved. She closed her hand on what seemed like an animal's pelt. Bracing her legs, she pulled a little man out by the beard. He made no sound, but looked at her out of big black eyes. She hoisted him over her shoulder and trotted downhill.

Her companions were streaming downhill, too. Each had caught at least one man. They carried them over their shoulders or tucked under their arms, or upside down, dangling by the ankles. One group of girls who had caught two men each had tied their nets together, stuffed their whole catch in, and were dragging the net downhill. The men struggled like herrings, trying to get to the center of the net bag because the outside ones were being bruised as they bumped over rocks.

While waiting for the first men to be brought in,
the girls of the scrub detail
flung off their tunics
and dived into the pool.

Nycippe took her man to the pool and was about to throw him to the scrub girls, but suddenly decided to bathe him herself. She carried him into the pool, and after ducking him a few times and swishing him back and forth in the water, she pulled him out and stretched him on a flat rock. She had taken sand from the bottom and now began to scour him. The dirt came off, but she kept scrubbing. A fierce curiosity had seized her; she felt she was unpeeling him to discover what was within. She scrubbed harder and harder, then saw that his skin was actually peeling off. He was in pain, she knew, but he made no outcry—although the other men in the pool were weeping and screaming as the girls worked on them.

"What am I doing wrong?" called Nycippe.

"You want to mix oil with the sand before scouring," said a scrub girl.

"No use bothering with that one anymore," said another. "Look at the poor thing. You might as well drown him."

Nycippe was rambunctious, but not really cruel. Now, she didn't recognize her feelings. She turned the little man in her hands to see how she had misused him. He looked like a half-flayed rabbit. He was a rabbit, and she felt herself turning into a leopard to rummage his bones. She saw the others looking at her, and knew they expected her to drown him.

She pretended to be pushing him under the water, but hid his face under her hand so that he could breathe. When the others were too busy to notice, she bore him to the shore and scooped some moss over him. He didn't say anything but his black eyes questioned her.

"You're not much to look at, but you've got guts," she whispered. "Maybe I can whip you into shape. Stay right here until I come back."

Now, Thyone had not let herself be lulled into carelessness while living happily with Malo. She had always suspected that the Amazons might come after their lost sister, and she had prepared against invasion. High up, near the mountain peak, she had arranged huge, round boulders, balancing them so that a slight shove would send them thundering down to crush anyone who might be climbing the slope.

Now, when the first sounds of the manhunt reached her cave, she snatched Malo up, set him on her shoulders, and raced toward the peak, letting him off only when they had reached the circle of rocks. She said, "I know you want to go down there and help your friends, my brave darling, but I won't let you."

"You won't?"

"Absolutely not. You'd never come back. One of the sisters will take you to Scythia and peel you like an onion to see where the song comes from."

Now, Malo's courage was confined to daring metaphors. The last thing he wanted to do was go down and fight. But he had always encouraged her to overestimate him. He heaved a deep sigh and said, "Very well, I'll stay up here—but only to please you."

"Oh, thank you, sweetheart."

In the pure hush of the mountaintop they heard faint screams drifting up from below. "Listen to them," said Malo. "They're having an awful time. I really should—"

She swung him off his feet and hugged him tightly to her. "You can't go! You promised! Anyway, you told me you write better about battles you haven't been to. Didn't you tell me that? Didn't you?"

"True, true," he murmured. "I shall want to write about this one, and had better not confuse myself with facts. Put me down now; you're breaking my ribs."

12

The Hippocrene Spring

The Amazons, coming from Scythia, had ridden up the northern slope of the mountain. Hercules, coming from Thebes, was mounting its steeper southern slope, and was unaware of what the warrior women were doing on the other side.

He climbed steadily, and it was hot work. Hera had bribed Apollo to swing his sun chariot low that day, and the land lay sweltering. Nor was it much cooler on the mountain. Hercules was parched. He had to drink, and soon. Nostrils quivering, he snuffed the wind like a horse and tried to pick up the scent of water. A faint, cool odor did drift to him. He strained his ears and heard a distant splashing. He turned off the path and made his way over rough ground to a natural cupping of rock. Here, from deep in the mountain, a spring spurted with such force that it made a plumed fountain. Flowers grew there, wild roses and iris and hyacinth, and the one known as heliotrope because it always turns to face the sun.

Hercules knelt and plunged his face in. It was the most delicious water he had ever drunk, ice cold, sparkling, tasting faintly of mint; it was like drinking some pure essence of earth. He had no way of knowing that this was the Hippocrene Spring,

Everything had changed. Colors pulsed.

whose coolness touched those who drank it with the incurable fever called poetry.

Hercules pulled his dripping face from the spring and gazed about in wonder. Everything had changed. Colors pulsed. Things presented themselves, insisting that he see them—a cypress, a berry bush, a soaring eagle, a goat far off. They uttered their names, and he heard them as if for the first time. This became a dance of names, seeming not only sound but colored music. The eagle he was watching became a white stallion balanced on golden wings, proclaiming the reliability of magic and the necessity for transformation—which poets know.

Hercules had drunk of the Hippocrene Spring and was becoming a poet. But he was unused to words and felt himself choking on a song unsung.

The fountain mist was making dim, gauzy rainbows, and Hercules couldn't quite see what had come to the other side of the spring. It was huge, a looming brightness. He stepped to one side and looked past the plume of water. He saw a stag, larger than any he had ever seen, and of a blinding whiteness. Its hooves were silver; its antlers were a candelabra of silver fire.

"A moon stag!" he said to himself. "Wandered away from the chariot. Artemis must be searching for him high and low. I shall catch it and bring it to her."

It was not a stag belonging to Artemis, although of the same breed, and it had always run free. But beginners in poetry are apt to prate wildly about the moon.

"Yes," thought Hercules. "Surely he is one of the team that draws the moon chariot across the night. And Artemis, maiden huntress, who swings the tides on a silver leash and hangs a torch for lovers, will thank me when I return this stag to her."

He thought these things, but could not say them. He didn't yet know how. In that big, superbly wrought body, poetry bypassed words and became action. And he began to chase the stag as it bounded away. The stag fled, became a white blur going up the hill. Hercules watched it race to the top, then bound over, to go down the other side.

"Terrific sprinter," thought Hercules. "We'll see how well he goes the distance."

But Hippocrene fever was coursing through his veins. He half forgot about the stag even while following it.

Some miles off Attica, a wedge-shaped head split the water. It was the serpent, Ladon, swimming toward the coast. Iole rode his head, her red hair snapping like a pennant behind her in the wind of their going.

Informed by the sea nymphs that Hercules was on Helicon, she had asked Ladon to take her there, without telling him why.

Ladon crawled ashore and began to undulate across Attica. His body moved by contraction like a giant worm, and he moved very fast. He was heading northward through the Peloponnese, then would angle northeast toward Thessaly, where Mount Helicon stood.

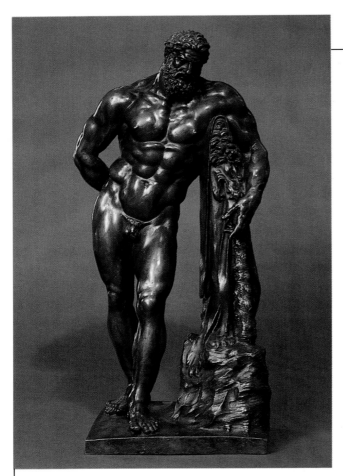

*Then they spotted
Hercules.*

Hercules ambled down the slope toward the encampment. Tall, suavely muscled young women milled about. Some were grooming horses. Some were in a pool, scrubbing little men who spluttered and wept. Others were sharpening swords against flat rocks. One group was playing with ropes, making their captives run and lassoing them as they ran. A pair of frolicsome twins, aglow with the excitement of their first raid, had tied their men to trees and were giving them a taste of the lash . . . not hitting hard—it was just an introductory flogging—the girls chatted and laughed as they swung their whips. Four Amazons were practicing archery with a human target. He was spread-eagled against the bole of a thick tree, and the women were shooting in turn. The idea was to come as close as possible without hitting him.

And the archers were so expert that arrows outlined his body but none had touched him.

Then they spotted Hercules. Saw a towering, bronzed, wide-shouldered youth wearing a lion skin and bearing an oaken club. They immediately stopped what they were doing and gaped in wonder. Their voices mingled.

"Look at him, would you? What a big one!"

"Can't be a man; must be a woman!"

"Must be, absolutely!"

"What does *she* want here?"

"She's on a raid of her own. Hurry, or she'll take the best ones."

"It's no woman!" bellowed Hippolyte. "It's a man, definitely."

"A man that big, can't believe it."

"Let's take him and throw the little ones back. He'd be more use than a mountainful of these runts."

"A prime cut! After him, girls!"

They shouted with eagerness, uttered war cries, beat sword against shield. The clamor came to Hercules like a dim murmur. He was trying to find a rhyme for tree and had forgotten why he was on the mountain. He waved absently to the ranks of warrior women, then wandered off, mumbling to himself.

Thinking always in terms of warfare, the sisterhood thought this stranger might be leading them into ambush and followed him warily. But, danger or no, they were determined to catch so fine a specimen.

"When I give the signal, we'll move in," called Hippolyte. "And don't forget, he's mine!"

No one answered, but every young Amazon there, except for Nycippe, had decided that Hercules must be hers alone, and was ready to fight Hippolyte for him.

13

The Silver Stag

era and Hecate hovered, watching. They had been pleased by the Amazons' campaign, delighted when they saw Hercules drinking of the spring, but were dismayed now as they saw him bounding down the mountain after a stag.

"I thought that springwater was supposed to do things to him," said Hera. "Scatter his wits, drain his strength. That's what you told me. But look at the brute. Look at him chasing that stag. He's tireless."

Indeed, as the stag raced down the mountain and onto the Thessalian plain, Hercules had put on speed and was managing to keep the animal in sight. He had no idea he was being pursued, but it didn't matter. For he was running faster than the Amazons could gallop their horses.

Furiously disappointed, the warrior women reined up and galloped back to retrieve their captives. But the battered poets had fled, finding holes and caves for themselves and burrowing so deep that the Amazons abandoned the search. They had been hunting listlessly anyway. The memory of the glorious big youth who had outrun their horses made these scruffy little cowards seem most unappetizing. As for the lost sister, Thyone, they had never even caught a glimpse of her. Hot and disgruntled, they trooped off the mountain and headed for Scythia—all but Ny-cippe; she had deserted.

In the darkest hour of night, she had gone to where she had hidden her captive, slung him across the withers of her horse and ridden toward the peak. She meant to find a cave and oil his cuts and bruises, and find out whether his silence meant song.

It was then that Ladon arrived, bearing Iole on his head, and began to climb the slope. The girl was wild with excitement. She stood up on the head to look about. She had come, finally, to the place where Hercules was supposed to be. Her gaze traveled up, up. She was at the foot of the mountain; its rock walls towered above her. He could be anywhere up there, or on the other side. She saw a flash of gold and stared in disbelief. A white horse was poised on golden wings, hanging between sky and peak. She was flooded with joy. She knew that wonders never came singly. Perhaps another wonder, the most wonderful of all, was about to happen . . . It did! A silver stag fled by, followed by Hercules running almost as fast.

She jumped off Ladon's head, crying, "Farewell!"

"What do you mean, 'farewell'?" asked Ladon.

"I must go now."

"Why?"

"To catch up with that man who just ran by."

"Why?"

"That's Hercules. He's why we've come here."

"Don't go."

"I must! I have something to tell him."

"What?"

"That's my affair! We're not married yet, you know. And never will be if you go on this way."

"What way?"

"All this hissy jealous stuff. 'Why . . . what . . . when . . .' It's unbearable!"

"You don't care for me then?"

"I do, I do, but I don't know how much. I have to go away to see if I care enough to come back."

She heard herself lying, she who had always been too much of her own girl to bother lying to anyone. But she would have said anything that would help her get away from the serpent and go to Hercules.

She saw a flash of gold and stared in disbelief.
A white horse was poised on golden wings,
hanging between sky and peak.

Hera and Hecate hovered invisibly over Hercules, watching him jump rocks and logs as he chased the stag. "Well," said Hera. "Why hasn't that ruffian been enfeebled by poetry, as you promised?"

"I made a slight miscalculation," said Hecate. "Hercules is a demigod. And I suppose poetry acts differently on him than on a mere mortal. It doesn't become song but a white-hot intellectual activity, igniting all his vital forces. But be easy, Hera. It's all happening for the best."

"The *best*!" cried Hera. "How can you claim that if he's getting stronger instead of weaker?"

"Patience, patience. Drinking of the Hippocrene Spring has suspended his judgment. He has forgotten about consequences, and has suddenly dropped everything to serve the moon. He will be chasing that stag across the wide earth, through the deepest valleys, over the highest mountains. It will flee and he will pursue. Such a chase must exhaust even a Hercules. And—I said this before, and I say it again—he will be easy prey for any monster you send against him."

Northward raced the stag, Hercules following, and Iole following him. And Ladon following all of them. The serpent didn't know what to do. He knew that Iole, unlike the others, would have to sleep some time, and he didn't know whether to stay with her and try to win her affection again, or to follow his enemy, Hercules.

"Perhaps she's lost her love for him in this grueling chase," thought Ladon. "If so, I won't have to kill him."

Therefore Ladon made himself go slowly, keeping the same distance behind Iole till he saw her finally fold herself beneath a tree and fall asleep. Moonlight sifted through the branches, making sequins of silver on the forest floor, and making him almost invisible as he crept toward the sleeping girl. He rose up on his coils and arched down to look upon her. In the gauzy moonlight she was the most beautiful thing he had ever seen. And love fought with murder in his untried heart.

He heard her voice. Was she awake? Was she speaking to him? He lowered his head close to her face, and saw that she slept. Was she speaking out of her sleep? Was she calling to him from that deep place where truth abides? That would be good, very good.

"Hercules," she moaned. "Oh, Hercules . . . Wait for me. Please?"

It was to be murder then; she had decreed it from her sleep. Ladon uncoiled and glided away, going much faster now. After several miles he caught sight of Hercules but did not attack. He was very confident of victory in the battle that was to come; nevertheless, he wished that that man, that entangler of young girls, that enemy, would exhaust himself running. Then he, Ladon, the patient one, the eternal waiter, the one who killed and fed at his own pleasure, would close in for the best kill of all— would drink the young Theban's blood and crack his bones.

At the very western edge of the world lay a small island that had been chosen for gigantic events. Here the Titan, Atlas, who had rebelled against Zeus, was condemned to stand forever, holding the sky on his shoulders. In happier times, he had wed a starry Titaness named Hespera, and she had borne him three beautiful daughters called the Hesperides. They had gone with their father to his place of punishment, had become apple nymphs, and guarded an orchard where grew a wondrous tree bearing golden fruit. This was the very tree that Ladon had wrapped himself about when he first climbed out of the sea and where he had first tasted human flesh.

And it was here, to the Island of the Hesperides, that the stag had come. Without pause, it had raced through Thessaly, northward through Thrace, through the land later to be called

Here the Titan, Atlas, who had rebelled against Zeus,
was condemned to stand forever,
holding the sky on his shoulders.

Rome and now called Italy, north again across mountains not yet called Alps, then through a fair, forested country that was to become France. Westward then, running as fast as it could, but beginning to slow down a bit—and all this time with Hercules still the same distance behind.

The stag came to an arm of the North Sea. It was as cold and choppy and foggy then as it is now under the name of the English Channel. Without hesitation, the stag leaped into the water and began to swim west.

Hercules had slowed down too now, and had not gained on the stag by the time he reached the water. He looked westward. A strong wind had begun to blow, sweeping the fog away. Across the water he saw dim white cliffs. He squinted, trying to locate the stag. Far off upon the water he spotted the silver gleam of its antlers.

He plunged into the channel. The icy water revived him. He began to swim very fast, faster than the stag was swimming, and had gained slightly on the animal by the time it reached shore. But when it did wade to the beach, it seemed as if it had been storing speed for a last sprint. One huge bound carried it over the sand past a fringe of trees, and it vanished. By the time Hercules reached shore the stag was nowhere to be seen.

He began to press inland, but was weary now. He had enjoyed the swim, but it exhausted him, and he knew he needed to rest before resuming the chase. Nor did he have any idea that he was upon the Utmost Isle. For the wind had dropped again, and an evening fog cloaked the figure of Atlas, so that it looked like a mountain peak.

Hercules slept, and awoke to a sunny morning. He arose immediately, swam in the sea, ate a handful of blackberries, and struck inland to search for the stag. All at once he found himself surrounded by three rosy young nymphs who joined hands and danced about him, singing:

Welcome, stranger,
welcome, man!
Don't try to leave us;
no man can!

"Greetings, lovely nymphs," he said. "Have you seen a silver stag?"

"No, but we have golden apples. We'll give them to you if you stay."

"I must go. I'm hunting that stag. It's somewhere on the island. But I'll come back when I've caught him, I promise. And we'll dance the night through."

"Daylight is fine for dancing too, almost as good as night. Dance now and hunt later."

"That cannot be."

"But you'll come back?"

"I always do what I promise—sooner or later."

Make it soon,
make it soon . . .
We'll dance up the sun,
dance down the moon . . .

"As soon as ever I may," said Hercules.

"Be careful of our father, though, sweet lad."

"He doesn't like us to have friends."

"When they come he starts avalanches."

"Who is your father?"

"Atlas is his name. There he is standing on that mountain, holding up the sky."

"That snowy peak?"

"It's not snow; it's his white beard."

"Farewell until I return," said Hercules.

He left the nymphs and went on his way, going through a grove and crossing a plain and coming to the foot of the mountain. He searched the slopes, trying to spot the stag. No matter how high it had climbed, its silver antlers, he knew, would catch the sun.

The mountain loomed. It rose and rose and ended in a plateau on which stood Atlas, legs braced, arms raised, holding the edge of the sky on his bowed shoulders. Hercules heard thunder rumble. But the sky was clear, and he realized that the Titan was calling down to him.

"What are you gawking at, little rat?"

"I come in peace," said Hercules.

"Depart in haste! I welcome no visitors. Have you come

to steal the golden apples?"

"No, My Lord."

"To steal my daughters?"

"Not that either."

"Well, you look like a thief, and thieves steal."

Atlas stamped his foot, dislodging a huge rock that tumbled down the mountain. Hercules sprang aside. The rock just missed him and buried itself in the earth.

"Begone, begone!" roared the Titan. "Or I'll stamp up an avalanche that will cover you in tons of rock."

"We have golden apples.
We'll give them to you if you stay."

73

*As soon as he touched shore,
the serpent thrilled with recognition.*

"He can't turn his head," thought Hercules, "or he'll shake the sky. I'll just go around behind him and search for the stag at the other end of the island."

But he was to find more than he wished on the other shore, for that was where Ladon had landed an hour before.

As soon as he touched shore, the serpent thrilled with recognition. This was the first island he had crawled upon when he had left the sea, ages before. Here was the first place he had eaten a meal that wasn't fish. That tree, gleaming afar . . . it was there he had couched until men and women came to eat its golden fruit, and he had eaten them. Remembering this, a savage craving for meat seized him . . . Live meat!

"I can eat what I want now," he thought. "She doesn't love me anymore."

He saw something else gleam. He couldn't tell what it was. He crept closer, and saw that it was a stag grazing. White fire glanced off its antlers; they were of pure silver, and its hooves were silver, too. But in between was a ton of venison, for the animal was huge.

Ladon circled, moving downwind, so that the stag could not pick up his scent. He crept closer. He was invisible against the grass. His entire length stiffened like a cable and became a blur of speed as he struck. His head was a battering ram, knocking the stag down. He opened his jaws and slowly engorged it. The head went in last, and it was still screaming as it vanished.

Ladon spat out the antlers, spat out the hooves, and crawled off to digest his meal.

14

Hero Meets Monster

Hercules, hunting the stag, saw a patch of white fire, and rushed forward. He stopped in horror as he saw the broken antlers on the ground, and the silver hooves. Where they lay, the grass was trampled and bloody.

When Hercules was priming for battle, he grew both hot and cold. The heat was rage coursing through his veins. At the same time, he was sheathed in coolness. Wit and thews were fusing, thought becoming action. He stood where he was and searched the meadow. Finally, he was able to distinguish the mottled coils of a serpent from the mingled light and shade where it lay. It seemed to be sleeping.

Hercules circled until he was downwind, then crept forward. He wanted to see whether the coils were bulging. They were.

"Yes," he said to himself. "The silver stag reposes in the belly of the beast. And now I shall prepare a bitter sauce for that meal."

Ladon awoke, and thrilled with ferocious glee to see Hercules coming toward him. But he pretended to be asleep still, and did not open his jaws, for he wanted his enemy to come within reach. Hercules kept creeping forward.

Ladon lashed out suddenly with his tail, a powerful, sweeping blow that could cave in the planking of a ship. Hercules saw the terrible tail scything at him, and leaped straight up, hacking down with his sword. But the serpent's scales were hard as armor plate; the blade skidded off.

Hercules fled. He dodged behind a tree as the tail swept back. He crouched low, letting the tail pass above his head and wrap itself about the thick bole. Hercules slipped away as the tree was wrenched, groaning, out of the earth. It came up, roots and all.

Ladon raised the tree like a club and smashed it down on Hercules' head. It could not dent his rocklike skull, but the blow drove him into the earth like a tent peg. At that moment, as Hercules was struggling to pull himself out of the hole, the serpent could have wrapped its tail about him and crushed him to death right there.

Instead, Ladon chose to whip about and come at him, jaws agape. Hercules snatched up the fallen tree and wedged it between the serpent's jaws. Ladon roared, swinging his head violently, trying to shake the tree out. But the sharp branches pierced the roof of his mouth.

He flailed about in agony, and Hercules had to dodge the sweeping tail. He saw now that the wedge wouldn't last. The serpent was biting down on it. Despite the agony, he was forcing his jaws together, crushing the tree. Hercules knew that if those jaws closed, they would spring open again, and close again—on him.

"He's bleeding," thought Hercules. "The roof of his mouth is bloody—must be the only place on his body not armored in leather. And this, perhaps, gives me one last chance."

Risking all, he sprang right into Ladon's mouth. Trying to balance himself on the slippery, heaving mass of the beast's tongue, he drove his sword upward, stabbing the unarmored

Ladon awoke, and thrilled with ferocious glee.

palate again and again. Now, the palate lies beneath the head. And the sword, driven with Hercules' last desperate strength, finally stabbed through the palate into the brain.

The serpent's eyes dulled. The great cable of its body went limp.

Hercules leaned on his sword and gazed down at the beast. It was dead. The stag was gone. The chase was ended. He was hungry and thirsty, and lusted for the orchard's fruit. He was cut and bruised, but nothing that frolicking in the moonlight with three luscious nymphs wouldn't cure.

He grinned up at the dim figure of Atlas. "I'll take them to the edge of the sea to dance," he said to himself. "And be able to dodge the avalanche by diving in."

The nymphs welcomed him joyously. They wreathed themselves about him, dancing up the sun, dancing down the moon. Their arms were smooth as apple blossoms, and their fragrance was of windfall apples. Atlas stamped furiously. But his daughters only laughed and made a dance of dodging rocks.

And Hercules, drunk on apple fragrance and blossoming touch and the whirling spirals of the dance, knew that he would have to leave at dawn or stay there forever, courting nymphs, dodging avalanches.

As if sensing what he felt, the Hesperides pressed closer. Their fragrance beat about him, and the hurtling rocks seemed harmless as falling blossoms. But the sky was flushing pink, shading to rose; there was a wash of lilac and a promise of hot gold. And he remembered a girl with a red mane of hair and jade green eyes and long ivory-brown arms and legs, and a tunic of lilac and rose.

"Farewell," he cried to the nymphs. He swept them into his arms and kissed each blooming face, kissed their crystal tears away. "Do not grieve; rejoice, rejoice! Others shall come to dance with you, my lovelies, and stay as long as you wish."

"Why are you leaving us? It must be for a girl."

"I have seven more monsters to face. And, in between, I must search for the girl who is searching for me."

He dived into the sea and swam eastward as dawn became day and the grieving voices of the Hesperides mingled with the cry of gulls.

Iole, being a daughter of the rainbow, whose home is the sky, could sometimes read the passage of birds and the pattern of stars for signs of what was to be.

When a black arrow of cranes crossed the sunset, and later that night was followed by a falling star, she knew that she must climb a cliff the next morning—for her destiny would move upon the waters.

She stood upon a cliff in Troezen and gazed out over the sea. Her hair was a red-gold pennant in the wind and her fluttering tunic was of lilac and rose. Far out, she saw something coming, and prepared to flee. For it was big, big; it could only be Ladon. Nevertheless, she waited until she could see it more clearly, then began to laugh and cry at the same time.

For it was a raft made of huge logs bound together, the slowest, clumsiest craft in the world, but it was scudding along like a canoe under the powerful strokes of a bronzed youth in a lion skin who was rowing with an uprooted tree.

She saw the raft swerve toward the beach, and she began to race down the cliff, her sobbing laughter turning to song as she ran to meet him.

As we have seen, monsters were not immortal; they could be slain by heroes and other monsters. But a dead one could always find employment with Hades. It took its place among his fiends and demons, and roamed the plain, terrorizing and mangling

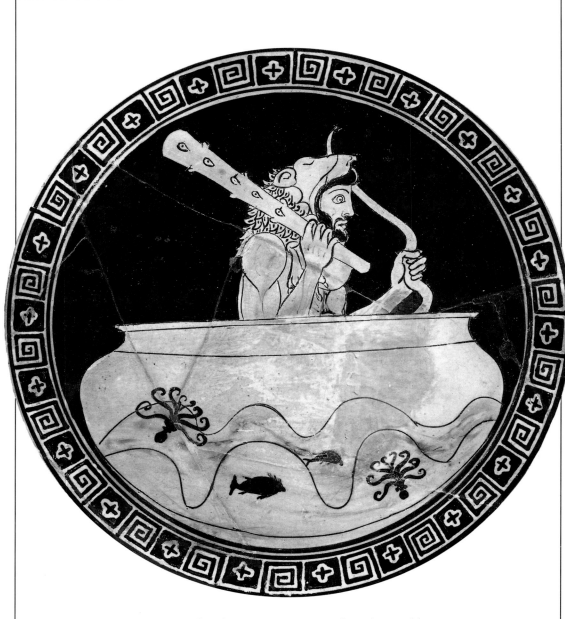

It was . . . the slowest, clumsiest craft in the world,
but it was scudding along like a canoe
under the powerful strokes
of a bronzed youth in a lion skin.

whomever it met, just as it had in life. For the theme of ancient Hell was that death changed nothing—and that hasn't changed either.

So it was that Ladon was welcomed into Tartarus. Although officially dead, he kept his hopes alive. He knew that Iole, being a demigoddess, was only half immortal, and that in a thousand years or so her shade would descend—and find him waiting, as he had waited since the beginning of time.

Acknowledgments

Letter Cap Illustrations by Hrana Janto

Cover, IOLE & LADON *(1989) by Hrana Janto, watercolor (10 3/8" × 12 3/4")*
  Courtesy of the artist

Opposite page 1, ADAM & EVE, *detail from the Sarcophagus of Adelphi (ca. 340)*
  Courtesy of the Museum of Archaeology, Syracuse
    Photo: Scala/Art Resource, NY

Page 3, *Detail from* THE SNAKE CHARMER *by Henri Rousseau (1844–1910), oil on canvas*
  Courtesy of the Jeu de Paume, Paris
    Photo: Scala/Art Resource

Page 4, *Detail from* THE MARRIAGE OF ZEUS AND HERA ON MT. IDA *(ca. 1st century* B.C.*)*
Roman mural
  Courtesy of the National Museum, Naples
    Photo: Scala/Art Resource

Page 6, SIREN, *detail from a mirror with a support in the form of a draped woman (mid–5th century* B.C.*), bronze (h. 16 1/8")*
  Courtesy of the Metropolitan Museum of Art, Bequest of Walter C. Baker (1972.118.78)

Page 10, DANTE'S VISION OF RACHEL AND LEAH *by Dante Gabriel Rosetti (1828–82), oil on canvas*
    Courtesy of the Tate Gallery, London
        Photo: John Webb/Art Resource, NY

Page 14, JUNO ASCENDING TO HEAVEN IN HER CHARIOT, *detail from* OVIDE MORALISÉ, *(ca. 14th century), a manuscript illuminated by Chretien Legouais*
    Courtesy of the Bibliothèque Municipale, Rouen
        Photo: Giraudon/Art Resource, NY

Page 16–17, LEVIATHAN, *two views, detail from an ivory jewel case (ca. 300 B.C.)*
    Courtesy of Museo Cristiano, Brescia
        Photo: Scala/Art Resource, NY

Page 18, EVE AND THE SERPENT *by Marc Chagall (1887–1985), stained glass window, Metz Cathedral*
        Photo: Giraudon/Art Resource, NY

Page 21, RAT SNAKE WITH DAYFLOWER PLANT *by Kitagawa Utamaro (1753?–1806), left half of plate X from* PICTURE BOOK OF SELECTED INSECTS *(Ehon Mushi Erabi) 2 vols., woodblock print, colors on paper (10 1/2" × 7 1/4" each page)*
    Courtesy of the Metropolitan Museum of Art, Rogers Fund, 1918 (JP 1052)

Page 23, GUARDIAN OF THE TREE *(ca. 1st century B.C.), fresco from Pompeii*
        Photo: Scala/Art Resource, NY

Page 26, MARS *by Diego Velásquez (1599–1660), oil on canvas*
    Courtesy of the Prado, Madrid
        Photo: Scala/Art Resource, NY

Page 29, THE GREAT BLACK AUROCHS *(ca. 15,000 B.C.), Cro-Magnon painting in Lascaux cave near Montignac, France*
        Photo: Art Resource, NY

Page 30, *Detail from* VENUS OF URBINO *by Titian (1490–1576), oil on canvas*
    Courtesy of the Uffizi Gallery, Florence
        Photo: Scala/Art Resource, NY

Page 32, ODYSSEA *by Jean-Auguste-Dominique Ingres (1780–1867), oil on canvas*
    Courtesy of Lyon Musée des Beaux Arts
        Photo: Scala/Art Resource, NY

Page 36, SELENE *(ca. 450 B.C.), Greek oenochoe in the beautiful style*
    Courtesy of the Archeology Museum, Florence
        Photo: Scala/Art Resource, NY

Page 38, PHILOKTETES ON LEMNOS *(ca. 430–420 B.C.), Greek red-figured vase (h. 6 1/8")*
    Courtesy of the Metropolitan Museum of Art, Fletcher Fund, 1956 (56.171.58)

Page 40, *Detail from black-figured Etruscan terra cotta vase (ca. 460 B.C.) by the Micali painter*
    Courtesy of the Museo Gregoriano, Vatican
        Photo: Scala/Art Resource, NY

Page 42, DIANA HUNTING *(ca. 4th century), sculptural relief, Roman copy of Greek original*
    Courtesy of Tempio Malatestimo, Rimini
        Photo: Scala/Art Resource, NY

Page 44, *Detail from* AMAZONS ARMING *(6th century B.C.), Attic amphora of Andokides*
   Courtesy of the Louvre, Paris
      Photo: Giraudon/Art Resource, NY

Page 46, KORE *(ca. 550–500 B.C.), Greek marble*
   Courtesy of the Acropolis Museum, Athens
      Photo: Nimatallah/Art Resource, NY

Page 48, *Detail from* METAMORPHOSIS *(ca. 14th century) from* OVIDE MORALISÉ, *illuminations by Chretien Legouais*
   Courtesy of the Bibliothèque Municipale, Rouen
      Photo: Giraudon/Art Resource, NY

Page 52, THREE AMAZONS STARTING FOR BATTLE *(ca. 465–460 B.C.) Greek red-figured vase attributed to the Mannheim painter (h. 13 1/8", dia. 9")*
   Courtesy of the Metropolitan Museum of Art, Rogers Fund, 1906 (06.1021.189)

Page 55, NYMPHS BATHING *(16th century), Italian print in the style of Parmigianino by unknown artist*
   Courtesy of the Metropolitan Museum of Art, Rogers Fund, 1922 (22.73.3-100)

Page 58, *Detail from* THE WATERFALLS, PISTIL MAWDDACH, NORTH WALES *by Samuel Palmer (1805–81), oil on canvas*
   Courtesy of the Tate Gallery, London
      Photo: John Webb/Art Resource, NY

Page 60, *Center detail from* WATERLILLIES *(version I) by Claude Monet (1840–1926), oil on canvas*
   Courtesy of L'Orangerie, Paris
      Photo: Giraudon/Art Resource, NY

Page 62, FARNESE HERCULES *(second half of 16th century) Florentine School bronze statuette*
   Courtesy of the National Gallery of Art, Washington, DC, Gift of Stanley Mortimer
      Photo: Art Resource, NY

Page 64, DIGESTION *(1989), sculpture by Dennis Oppenheim, wax, deer, copper gas line (5' × 2' × 4')*
   Courtesy of the artist

Page 67, PEGASUS *by Albert Pinkham Ryder (1847–1917), oil on canvas*
   Courtesy of the Smithsonian Institution, Washington, DC
      Photo: Scala/Art Resource, NY

Page 70, ATLAS I *(1989) by Earl Staley, acrylic on canvas (22" × 33")*
   Courtesy of the artist

Page 73, THE THREE GRACES *by Raphael (1483–1520), oil on canvas*
   Courtesy of the Musée Condé, Chantilly
      Photo: Giraudon/Art Resource, NY

Page 74, THE LAIR OF THE SEA SERPENT *by Elihu Vedder (1836–1923), oil on canvas (12" × 30")*
   Courtesy of the Metropolitan Museum of Art, Gift of Mrs. Harold G. Henderson, 1976 (1976.106.1)

Page 76, HERCULES AND TRITON, *detail from terra cotta bowl (ca. 500–450 B.C)*
   Courtesy of the Tarquinia Museum, Italy
      Photo: Nimatallah/Art Resource, NY

BOOKS BY BERNARD EVSLIN

Merchants of Venus
Heroes, Gods and Monsters of the Greek Myths
Greeks Bearing Gifts: The Epics of Achilles and Ulysses
The Dolphin Rider
Gods, Demigods and Demons
The Green Hero
Heraclea
Signs & Wonders: Tales of the Old Testament